The Seventies

John Banks

Photography by G H F Atkins

Venture publications

Front cover and below: The appearance of public road transport in many British towns and cities underwent a radical change in the 1970s, due in no small part to the formation of the National Bus Company on 1st January 1969. The scene in Brighton became perhaps more colourful than it had been. Brighton Corporation had changed its livery from red and cream to blue and white a decade or so earlier than these June 1972 views, though it took a while for the red and cream to disappear. A more profound change involved the local Tilling operator (another red and cream fleet), Brighton Hove & District, whose operation passed into Southdown control once both were part of the NBC. Southdown, however, retained BH&D's livery and fleetname, as shown in these pictures of Northern Counties-bodied Daimler Fleetlines. Southdown's Leyland PD3 Titans in the former BET operator's classic green and cream, were the most stable element facing the observer in 1972.

Rear Cover: **UCS 621** had been new to Western SMT in 1963. An Alexander-bodied 71-seat Albion Lowlander, it was transferred to Walter Alexander & Sons (Fife) Ltd as **FRE36** in February 1967 and was sold for scrap in 1978.

Title page: The transformation of the appearance of its coaching fleet by the NBC, involving the supression of dozens of constituent company liveries, and their replacement by a variety of versions of a corporate image, is well shown in this picture taken at Wellington Street coach station, Leeds, in March 1975. The all-over white for long-distance intercity routes is evident on West Yorkshire and Ribble vehicles, and the "local coach" livery is seen in two versions: blue and white on an East Yorkshire Marshall-bodied Leyland Leopard; and poppy-red and white on a West Yorkshire Bristol RE and a Ribble Leyland Leopard.

The former BET and Tilling company operators in our period were all under the auspices of the National Bus Company, but for some years from 1969 their origins remained evident. There were, too, some interesting juxtapositions of livery as the NBC gradually imposed its corporate image. In August 1973, at Mansfield, Midland General **752** (**YNU 351G**), a Bristol FLF6G Lodekka dating from 1968, still in original livery, contrasts with No. **683** (**447 SNU**), an FSF6G Lodekka, which had succumbed to poppy-red and white. Both passed to Trent in October 1976 and 752, a 70-seater, was later sold for preservation. It is a regular visitor to rallies in the Midlands and is kept in pristine Midland General original livery. The 60-seat FSF was withdrawn and sold for scrap in October 1977.

A writer on transport - or, for that matter, on any subject wherein nostalgia plays its part - who is not a professional historian can easily fall into the way of viewing matters subjectively, calling down upon his head criticism when he neglects to delve deeply enough to find the commercial or technical justifications (if such exist to *be* found) behind the ripples and waves that have over the years beset - often changing beyond recognition: seldom leaving totally unchanged - the things he has known and loved.

The question of "the golden age" comes into it, as does the amorphous feeling that "fings ain't wot they use' ter be" and one often hears talk of "the good old days when things were done properly" and, more forthrightly, "there ought to be a law against messing things up like this".

Surely a lot to do with the strength of such feelings must relate to those hobbies and interests that were with us in our childhood and formative years and - important, this - *remained* with us into maturer years. When, therefore, the younger enthusiasts chide we greybeards for living in the past, we can smile knowingly, secure in the knowledge that in the year 2050 they will look back through *their* rose-tinted spectacles upon the Optares, Dennis Darts and Volvos with which they are growing up just as avidly and wistfully as those of us more stricken in years muse longingly on Arabs, Titans and Regents.

For a long time nothing seemed to change: our local operators withdrew buses, yes, and - certainly - they bought new ones, but homogeneity was not affected and they stayed the same colour. What can now be perceived as small changes - reversed liveries, underfloor-engined single-deckers, tentative early attempts at driver-only operation, and so on - pale into insignificance beside major upheavals such as the founding of the National Bus Company.

That cataclysmic event took place on 1st January 1969 and there followed in rapid order the PTEs: although we knew what was coming, none of us - including, one suspects, many employed in the industry - really knew exactly *what* was coming. The nineteen-sixties petered out with little or no change: well, red or green wheels instead of black, perhaps, and other insignificant cosmetic details; and as the seventies dawned one could have been forgiven for wondering why one had been worrying. That decade, however, was to stand the passenger-carrying road transport industry on its head and by the middle of it we on the sidelines who had no inside knowledge could not but stand by and realise that our nebulous fears of 1969 had fallen far short of the reality of 1975.

Similar disturbances of the equilibrium - the involvement in the late 1920s of the railways in bus companies, the rigours of wartime operation, the creation of the British Transport Commission in 1948 - had been perhaps less well recorded on film than was the 1969 change and - more to the point as far as this volume is concerned - by the latter year affordable colour photography of potentially excellent quality was a commonplace.

The seventies was a decade of change in other ways than that of the NBC's consolidation across the land and the PTEs in the conurbations. The rear-engined double-decker had been with us not just since the sixties but since the decade before that; yet recent traditional forward-engined buses (the last had been built in 1969) were, in a way, reassuringly, still among those present. Reassuringly only "in a way" because, while half-cab double-deckers might well have been traditional, some of the liveries in which they were appearing as the seventies gathered momentum were anything but traditional. Midland Red buses in West Midlands PTE livery, the Manchester and Stockport fleets in SELNEC colours and Notts & Derby Lodekkas in National Bus Company red will suffice as examples of what is meant here.

The correspondence pages of enthusiast club newsletters have been known to resound to the plaints of the "super sixties" and "sad seventies" (or *vice versa*) brigades, each bewailing the other's lack of right-thinkingness. These standpoints bring us back to the point made in the first paragraph of these notes: subjectivity. But: how to be objective? *Can* we, with neither political nor industry axe to grind, answer these questions objectively?

Why, for instance, *was* it necessary to destroy - no! "destroy" is too emotive a word to be classed as objective: let us rather say "dismantle and reassemble" - London Transport? Why did the NBC have to change Tilling red and green for different shades of the same colours? One could perhaps accept, objectively, the case for the national coaching system having a corporate image, but why did buses operating in local areas many hundreds of miles apart and never impinging the one upon the other have to be the same colour, thus losing their users the superb liveries of East Yorkshire, City of Oxford and Midland General, to name but three? Why were the municipalities, with their long traditions of tailor-made local services, responsive to neighbourhood needs, known and understood by their patrons, deemed incapable of continuing to serve their communities? And why and how were the monolithic PTEs thought better able to provide such service?

In a magnificent *non sequitur*, the writer proposes not attempting to answer those questions, for he freely admits to not knowing the answers - or, rather, could answer them from the subjective viewpoint, but that would be self-defeating in the present context.

Where objectivity *can* come in is in a simple examination of what actually happened in the seventies: Tilling red or green became poppy-red or leaf-green; the former BET and Tilling coaching vehicles became all-over white (and - objectivity be damned - if anybody thinks that *that* was an improvement...); many municipalities disappeared, subsumed into the PTEs, their liveries changed, their routes altered and renumbered, staff conditions affected for good or bad, passengers confused - at least temporarily. And can one be sure that it all *was* "a good thing", "a change for the better"? These events are not more than three decades in the past but where are the PTEs and the NBC today? If they were the universal panacea why are they not still with us? Was their disappearance in favour of deregulation and privatisation "a good thing" etc., etc.? To attempt an answer to that, however, would move us beyond our period here, which is and must remain 1970 to 1979.

For the contents of these pages the criterion has been that the pictures must have been taken in those years, so we are offering a look at what was running, of whatever age, and not simply just what was new. We have tried to delineate the change from old to new with some of the intermediate stages for good measure. And, of course, subjectivity has won hands down, for the presentation concentrates unashamedly on what was being lost rather than what was replacing it.

Acknowledgements and bibliography

Every photograph in the book and on its covers was taken by G H F Atkins, a friend of the writer for around 40 years. Geoffrey is certainly among the finest transport photographers this country has seen: recalled with pleasure are joint photographic sessions with him in Nottingham as late as 2001 and 2002 whose results maintain his very high standards; it was salutary to realise that those sessions took place fully three quarters of a century since Geoffrey had exposed his first negative of a bus (at Skegness in 1927). Now in his 92nd year, Geoffrey has passed his collection to friends in recent years, including many items to the writer, and it is a privilege to once again be able to share his splendid colour work with the enthusiast reader. An earlier book in the *Colour Prestige Series* covered the 1960s.

As so often the writer has shamelessly pestered Ron Maybray, another friend of four decades, for confirmation of vehicle dates and details culled from Ron's impeccable and amazingly informative written records. The cumulative debt is incalculable, can never be repaid, and is again acknowledged with great gratitude. Philip Battersby and John D Watson have over the years patiently answered many questions whose answers have helped shape this and other books. David and Mary Shaw and John Senior have read the pages in proof form to the immense benefit of the book.

The publications of The PSV Circle and The Omnibus Society are never far away when a work such as this is being prepared. We should be lost without them and another great debt is herewith once more acknowledged.

In addition, the following books were consulted in preparing and checking some of the captions and are recommended to readers wishing to know more about this period of Britain's passenger transport history:

Akehurst, L & Stewart, D: London Country. 2001, Capital Transport.
Banks, J & Atkins, G: Crosville. 2001, Venture Publications.
Gray, P, Keeley, M & Seale, J: Midland Red 1940 to 1970. 1979, TPC.
Green, O & Reed, J: The London Transport Golden Jubilee Book. 1983, The Daily Telegraph.
Keeley, M: Buses in Camera - English PTEs. 1979, Ian Allan.
Roberts, D: Bristol RE - 40 Years of Service. 2002, NBC Books.

John Banks
Romiley, Cheshire
May 2003

Motor bus operation in Leicester commenced in 1924, and in 1974 its golden jubilee was celebrated by Leicester City Transport. Leyland PD3/1 Titan No. **164** (**TBC 164**) was repainted for the occasion in Leicester's original motor bus livery. The Willowbrook-bodied 74-seater is seen in July of that year with, in the background and representing the operator's then current livery, No. **266** (**PJF 266M**), a Metropolitan (MCW-built using Scania running units), which had been new the previous April.

AEC Reliance **JJF 1E**, a 51-seat coach with Plaxton Panorama I body, which was in the fleet of Straws of Leicester, heads a line of vehicles offering tours and excursions. Another Straws Reliance is alongside, and vehicles from the Barton and Midland Red fleets are among the remainder. The location is Humberstone Gate, Leicester, and the date August 1971. Straws were offering a trip to Alton Towers for 60 pence while Barton was hoping for custom to Twycross Zoo.

Matlock bus station in the summer sunshine of July 1972 was home to what has the outward appearance of a traditional scene, but which betrays some recent and far-reaching changes.

Of the three identifiable vehicles, two are ex-the North Western Road Car Company. **SJA 345J**, on the left, was a Bristol RELL6G with Marshall 49-seat front-entrance bodywork. As North Western No. 345, it had been new in 1971. It had been in Trent colours as fleet number **330** since March 1972 and after withdrawal by Trent served as transport for a marching band. In November 1992 it was rescued for preservation.

The other ex-North Western vehicle, on the right of the picture, was **AJA 141B**, the former NWRCC No. 141, a Leyland PSU3/3RT Leopard new in 1963. It had an Alexander 49-seat coach body and was running as Trent No. **299**. In 1977 it was exported to an Eireann operator, King of Galway, and reregistered 4413 IM. It finished its days as a storeshed at Ballyglunin.

8625 DT in the blue livery of J H Woolliscroft (Silver Service), of Darley Dale, was a 45-seat front-entrance Roe-bodied AEC Reliance. New to Doncaster Corporation as No. 25 in November 1961, it was sold to Woolliscroft in 1970 and used until September 1973.

The unmistakeable Sheffield skyline forms an impressive backdrop to a May 1970 view of Pond Street bus station, in which traditional, forward-engined vehicles survive among - and even, in this case, outnumber - rear-engined machines. The only identifiable vehicle, seen parked behind two Leyland Atlanteans, is No. **1334** (**6334 WJ**), a 1960 Roe-bodied 64-seat AEC Regent V with rear entrance and platform doors. Six months after passing to the South Yorkshire PTE in April 1974, the AEC was scrapped.

Above: This might be merely three decades in the past - but what nostalgia! The coach park at Windermere in May 1974 was host to a remarkable selection of independent coaches on AEC, Bedford, Ford and Leyland chassis carrying bodywork - as far as can be made out - from Duple or Plaxton, the two major suppliers to the private sector. Most sizes of coach then allowed are present, from small Bedford VAS 29-seaters to maximum dimension vehicles seating upwards of 50. Vehicles of Abbeyways Mini Coaches, of Halifax (the two Bedford VASs) and York Pullman (in the right foreground) are identifiable; and an AEC Reliance - in grey and red livery - looks like HFV 757E, of Abbotts of Blackpool. The green and white Leyland Leopard in the centre, alongside the grey hut, has the fleetname "LEEDS". The family cars are not without interest, either, and range from Ford Anglia to Mercedes.

Right: The Bedford SB was very popular with independents. **179 MVO** was No. **79** in the fleet of South Notts, of Gotham. It had been new in May 1962, had a Duple 41-seat body, and was the SB8 version, signifying the fitting of a Leyland engine. It was at Broad Marsh, Nottingham in February 1970 and was withdrawn in 1975.

11

Above: Although new to East Kent after it passed to the NBC, this Plaxton-bodied AEC Reliance 49-seater has a pleasing traditional appearance. One of a batch of six, the vehicle was new in 1970 and was withdrawn in 1982. East Kent did not use fleet numbers until later in the 1970s. **VFN 38H** was at Victoria Coach Station in September 1970. Withdrawn in late 1982, it subsequently served four owners in Devonshire.

Right: The story of exiled London buses would need (indeed, has had) several complete books to tell. London Transport frequently disposed of buses that had not reached the end of their economic life and many units from the RT, RTL and RTW classes were happily acquired by smaller operators, including many an independent, among them Astill & Jordan Ltd, of Ratby, Leicester, who put **KXW 22** into service in

October 1965. A Leyland version of the RT type, based on the Titan PD2, this bus had been new to London Transport in 1950 as RTL672. It was withdrawn in June 1972 and is reported still in existence as late as 1998. It was photographed at Leicester in August 1970.

Johnson, of Rushden, ran **GRP 187D**, a 1966 Bedford VAM14 with Duple 45-seat coachwork. In May 1972 it was on private hire work in London and was caught in the frame when AEC Regent **ST922** (**GJ 2098**) was photographed *(see also next page)*. The ST was ex-Thomas Tilling, London Transport and a Hertfordshire scrapyard, and had been totally refurbished by LPC Coachworks, of Hounslow, for the pioneer preservationist Prince Marshall.

The London Routemaster, in production since 1958, might have been thought of as rather venerable by the end of the seventies. That hundreds are still in service in the new millennium speaks volumes for the soundness of the original design and the quality of maintenance and refurbishment subsequently applied to them. Many have been scrapped, though, including these two in 1986/7. **RM2105 (ALM 105B)** is seen in May 1972, and **RM131 (VLT 131)** *(>> opposite page)* was at Kings Cross in September 1978. The seventies saw a small but visually important change - typified by RM131 - whereby the LONDON TRANSPORT fleetname transfer was replaced by a white circle-and-bar logo.

The Routemaster was the last bus to be designed specifically for London service by the operator - a prototype appeared at Chiswick Works in 1954 and was running in public service by 1956 and, as we have seen, production versions came in 1958. The next generation of London bus should have been the FRM - a front-entrance, rear-engined version of the Routemaster; only one prototype was built however, and the new London double-decker would be sourced on the open market. The reasons for such a sweeping change are too complicated to go into in a short caption; certainly politicians were involved, as was the unwise, ill-conceived push towards universal driver-only operation - something thankfully not yet achieved in London. The new bus was based on the Daimler Fleetline chassis, following experimental batches of both Fleetlines and Leyland Atlanteans in 1965/6. Two of the earliest of the new Fleetlines, **DMS10/32** (**EGP 10/32J**), are seen in May 1971. They had Gardner engines and Park Royal 68-seat dual-doorway bodywork. Both had entered service the previous January. Significantly, both were withdrawn and scrapped before either of the Routemasters illustrated on pages 16/7. There were 136 of this first series, registered EGP 1-136J, and very few of them survived into second ownership, most going for scrap in 1980-2, being long outlived by hundreds of the RMs they were meant to replace. The small black and white logos on the front panels indicated a coin-slot fare-collection system.

DMS1852 (GHM 852N) came in May 1975 and was photographed at Victoria in the following September. Driver-only operation of the busy 10A between Victoria and Aldgate is better imagined than carried out. In this case the bodywork, to similar specification, was by Metro-Cammell. DMS1852 was withdrawn in 1983, used as a driver-trainer and sold for scrap in early 1990.

Above: If the Daimler Fleetline left something to be desired as a standard double-decker for the rough-and-tumble of operation in the Capital, the rear-engined AEC Swift single-decker was possibly even more of a headache. The first examples (known in London as AEC Merlins) had appeared in 1966 for the inauguration of the revolutionary Red Arrow flat-fare, coin-in-the-slot, short-haul routes in central London. Those early examples had had rather angular bodywork by Strachans. A later version by Park Royal is seen on **SMS300** (**EGN 300J**) in suburban surroundings in May 1971. The body had 33 seats and two doors, the second "S" in its fleet classification indicating that many passengers were expected to stand. This vehicle, new in January 1971, was withdrawn from passenger service in 1983, transferred to the non-passenger fleet, sold to a dealer for spares in 1986 and finally broken up in 1990.

Right: A surprising purchase in the mid 1970s was a batch of 164 dual-doorway, 72-seat Metropolitans, built by Metro-Cammell using Swedish Scania Vabis running units. Known as the MD class, they were sprightly performers but did not last. Twenty-one of them - including **MD8** (**KJD 208P**) shown here at Kings Cross in September 1978 - were sold in 1983 to Reading Corporation to join the 33 similar buses already in that operator's fleet.

Above: The Transport (London) Act 1969 was the cause of great change to bus and coach operation in the Capital in the seventies. From 1st January 1970 the GLC gained control of London Transport operations broadly within its own area, and ownership of Green Line and Country Area was given to the National Bus Company, which had been in existence since 1st January 1969. London Country Bus Services Ltd, as the new operation was named, was by 1973 putting Leyland Nationals to work on Green Line routes. Initially fitted with typical spartan interiors, they graduated to moquette covered seats and later examples had luggage racks and seats with high backs. **SNC118** (**WPG 218M**) was one of the latter. It entered service in 1974 and is seen at Aldgate in September 1975. Also in the picture are **DMS816** (**TGX816M**) and two RMLs (the 30ft-long version of the Routemaster), one of which - **RML2730** (**SMK 730F**) dating from 1967 - is at the time of writing still in active service with Arriva London South.

Right: As great a contrast with the bustle of bus operation in London as might be imagined is afforded by these two Guy Wolfs of Llandudno UDC. **JC 9736** dated from 1949 and had a Barnard 21-seat body; **AJC 551**, a Metalcraft-bodied 24-seater, was new in 1951. They were photographed in July 1970.

In an age of ever-increasing standardisation of vehicle types and liveries - be it of the Tilling and BET companies before 1969 or those of the National Bus Company afterwards - sometimes tending towards a certain blandness in appearance, the Scottish operators provided rich fare for the enthusiast's camera. These views of vehicles from the Walter Alexander & Sons (Fife) Ltd fleet were taken in Kirkcaldy in July 1971. The Lodekka *(above)* was an LD6G model with 60-seat Eastern Coach Works bodywork. **OMS 237** was new in May 1960 to Walter Alexander & Sons Ltd, of Falkirk, as fleet number RD134. After transfer to the Fife fleet on 15th May 1961 it was numbered **FRD134**. The vehicle was sold for scrap in 1977. Daimler Fleetline **FRF2** (**LXA 402G**) *(right)* was a 1968 CRG6LX Gardner-engined model, with 75-seat bodywork by Alexander. It was numerically the second of a batch of 20 that, after a number of years of Bristol orders, were the first rear-engined double-deckers in the Fife fleet. LXA 402G was sold to a dealer in 1983 and there is no known record of any further owner.

Outwardly similar Scottish coaches betray on closer inspection considerable differences. The Walter Alexander & Sons (Fife) Ltd vehicle shown above was an AEC Reliance dating from 1963. **FAC19 (AXA 219A)** was fitted with the ubiquitous Alexander Y-type coachwork, with 41 seats and a manually operated inward opening door. One of 14 delivered in that year, it later became transport for farm workers and was despatched to a breaker in Carnoustie in 1982. It was photographed in Perth in July 1971. On the opposite page is shown Walter Alexander & Sons (Northern) Ltd's **NT40** (**VRG 140L**). Whereas the Fife AEC Reliance was of the more substantially engineered "heavyweight" category of chassis generally favoured by the larger company operators, VRG 140L was a Ford R1114, of the "lightweight" type (mainly built by Ford or Bedford) less often found in such fleets and more favoured by the independent sector. A 1972 vehicle, the Alexander coachwork was for 49 passengers and the door was a power-operated two-piece affair. This coach passed to Highland Transport in 1977 and was withdrawn in 1983, after which nothing is known of it. The vehicle was photographed in Nottingham, with a very long journey ahead of it, in June 1975

Above: A contemporary of the Alexander Northern Ford shown on the previous page, and photographed at the same place in the same month, was Eastern Scottish **ZH539** (**BSG 539L**), a Leyland Leopard PSU3/3R with very similar Alexander 49-seat coachwork: minor visible differences are the split windscreen as opposed to the one-piece unit on the Ford and the side and indicator lamp clusters. New in 1973,

BSG 539L was withdrawn in 1984 and was later noted working for a farmer in the Malton area.

Right: Despite its many fine designs and the undoubted excellence of its products, the British coachbuilding industry could seldom be accused of being sensational. Something not far from a sensation, however, was caused by the 12-metre M-type coachwork, with its hint of American Greyhound practice, from Alexander in 1968 for

the Scottish Bus Group's London express services. Initially fitted to the Bristol REMH6G chassis, after the latter's demise the M-type appeared on some Volvo B58s, of which Western SMT's No. **2541** (**HSD 712N**), a 1975 42-seat, toilet-equipped machine, is shown here at Newark. After withdrawal it worked for Black Prince, Morley, reregistered 6571 WF; later, in 1990, it was converted as a stock-car transporter.

In July 1979, 75 years of Midland Red were being celebrated by Daimler Fleetline No. **6007** (**GHA 407D**), a 1966 Alexander-bodied 77-seater. It was at Coventry on a special service to the Stoneleigh showground. 6007 was scrapped in 1984.

The magnificent Midland Red D9 double-decker is represented by No. **5402** (**BHA 402C**) of 1965, seen at Leicester. The BMMO/Willowbrook body had 72 seats and platform doors. After withdrawal it was sold for scrap in August 1977. A sign of the times in this August 1973 picture is the poppy-red livery and double-N arrow logo of the National Bus Company.

Above: Midland Red coaches were, like its service buses, often built in-house: demand sometimes outstripped capacity, however, and then vehicles were purchased from proprietary manufacturers. In 1965, 49 Leyland PSU3/4R Leopards entered service equipped with Duple Northern 49-seat Commander coachwork. The batch was CHA74-122C, and we illustrate **CHA 100C**, which had BMMO fleet number 5800, and which in March 1976 was transferred to National Travel (South West) as fleet number 209. Later, in July of that year, it moved again, to Greenslades, of Exeter, as No. 260. The picture was taken at Victoria coach station in May 1971.

Right: The circumstances in 1970 in which Leyland Leopards were again purchased were rather different, in that by then Midland Red had ceased building its own vehicles. The vehicle shown, **6243** (**WHA 243H**), was a PSU3A/4R with Plaxton Panorama coachwork - a surprising reversion, as Midland Red already had examples of the more modern Plaxton Elite in its fleet. 6243 was one of a batch of 30 (WHA 226-55H), which entered service between May and August 1970 as Midland Red's LC11 class. After sale to an independent, 6243 was rebodied (by Duple) and reregistered MNY 892X. In this view it was at the Goose Fair, Nottingham, in October 1971.

Above: The Panorama design from Plaxton in a slightly earlier incarnation was distinguished (or disfigured in the opinion of some) by a thick decorative metal band round the waistrail from the end of the first bay forwards. This style of coachwork appeared in the Midland Red fleet on a batch of 16 Leyland PSU4/4R Leopards in 1966. As originally built they were 36-seaters for extended tour work but the seating was later increased to 42. The first of the batch, **5824 (GHA 324D)**, which had entered service in July 1966, was still a 36-seater when photographed outside the buffet bar at the south-east side of

Victoria coach station in September 1972. Number 5824 was converted as a towing wagon in 1977, in 1988 was reregistered Q141 VOE, and sold for scrap in 1997.

Right: Not yet mentioned in our survey of the decade, the Passenger Transport Executives (universally known as the PTEs) were a 1970s phenomenon that wrought a change fully as traumatic as that brought about by the NBC. The West Midlands PTE was formed on 1st October 1969 from the municipal operations of Birmingham, Walsall, West Bromwich and

Wolverhampton. Midland Red services within the PTE's area were acquired in December 1973 and a number of single- and double-deck buses were transferred. Of a batch of 33 Daimler CRG6LXB Fleetlines with Alexander 75-seat dual-doorway bodies that entered service in 1970/1 with Midland Red as part of the DD13 class, no fewer than 25 passed to the WMPTE. One of them was No. **6161 (YHA 261J)** - the first of the batch - seen here in Birmingham in August 1977 in West Midlands livery. After withdrawal, this vehicle was sold for scrap in April 1982.

Above: In 1970/1 Crosville Motor Services bought 100 Seddon RU chassis fitted with Seddon bodies, a move that the company probably regretted. They managed between ten and twelve years from them, although contemporary criticism levelled at these vehicles might cause one to wonder how they did it. Fifty of the Seddons were 45-seat dual-door buses and 50 were dual-purpose 47-seaters. The "dual-purpose" concept was perhaps being stretched here: it normally required more than a token gesture towards coach-like standard of seating and appointments and it was widely felt that these Seddons made no such gesture. In the end Crosville decided - or were forced to the conclusion - that it had 100 unusable and unsaleable buses on its hands, but that a use might be found for their Gardner engines. Thus 98 of the engines were removed and fitted into Leyland Nationals. **SPG796 (OFM 796K)**, one of the 45-seaters, was in Llandudno in September 1972. It was scrapped in 1981.

Right: The same month and place for Crosville's smart 1965 Bristol FLF6B Lodekka **DFB199 (DFM 201C)**. The 70-seat Eastern Coach Works body was resplendent in a new coat of Tilling green paint. The vehicle was withdrawn and scrapped in 1978.

Above: Crosville also achieved more years of service from this Bedford VAM70 than the larger company operators normally did from their lightweight chassis. **CVF694** (**XFM 694G**) had a Duple 45-seat body, was new in 1969 and sold for scrap in February 1980. It was one of a batch of four, two of which went after withdrawal to operators in the Irish Republic. It seems odd that this one and CVF692 were scrapped at only eleven years of age. No doubt they had been well used, but they were also well maintained and would have been a bargain for an independent. The vehicle was photographed on a tour to Bodnant Gardens, North Wales, in July 1970.

Right: The Eastern Coach Works-bodied Bristol MW6G was a much more substantial vehicle than the Bedford. Crosville's **CMG473** (**2178 FM**) was a 39-seater, which had been new in 1963, was reclassified for stage-carriage work in 1976 and sold for scrap in 1978. Crosville's cream and black coach livery was a good example of effectiveness achieved through simplicity. CMG473 - one of the large batch CMG467-92 - was at Llandudno in July 1970.

Above: Five years into the National Bus Company at Llandudno in September 1974, a Crosville driver stands in the late-summer sun, studiously ignoring the photographer as this view was recorded of **CMG520 (7622 FM)**, a 1964 Bristol MW6G with Eastern Coach Works 39-seat front-entrance coachwork. The livery is the version of the NBC's local coach colours as applied to vehicles of the former green Tilling fleets. This vehicle was withdrawn in 1976 and sold to an independent operator based in Maenclochog.

Right: Sales of time-served vehicles from former Tilling NBC fleets occasionally produced surprises, perhaps none greater than when ex-BET Yorkshire Woollen found itself running obsolete Bristol KSW double-deckers. Less unusual, in that United's staff would have been familiar with the type, was the July 1976 move from Crosville to United of SMG390 (**306 PFM**), another ECW-bodied Bristol MW6G 39-seater, this time dating from 1960. As United **2304** it was noted by the writer in Scarborough running in green livery but was later put into the NBC's poppy red. It was at Ripon in June 1977 and was withdrawn the following November.

Above: This United Automobile Services Bristol RELL6G, an ECW-bodied 53-seater, was new in 1968 as R87 (**THN 887F**), and had been renumbered **4187** (on 1st January 1969) by the time of this September 1978 view at Harrogate. After withdrawal it was sold in October 1980 to Citybus, Belfast, and was maliciously destroyed in civil disturbances in March 1988. At around that time, Citybus bought in many second-hand REs for use on routes where such disturbances were prevalent: nearly all of them were destroyed.

Right: At the well-known Corner Café terminus in Scarborough, United's No. **709** (**PUF 590R**) waits to depart on the short sea-front service in September 1977. From 1926 to 1968 there had been special buses built for use on this largely tourist service - from canvas-topped Daimlers, through Plaxton-bodied ADCs and Leyland Tigers to lengthened Bristol L5Gs with a bus-seated version of the ECW fully fronted coach body; thereafter whatever vehicles could be found - and they were often less than perfectly suited to such work - were used. As its registration mark suggests, this VR had been intended for the Southdown fleet. Transferred to Tees & District in February 1990, it was scrapped in March 1992.

Above: The seventies saw the NBC finding its feet and attempting to make the best use of its assets across an operating area that was the largest ever to have been under one management in the British Isles. That included moving surplus vehicles around as required, which resulted in some strange liveries appearing: for example, green Lodekkas in the United fleet. This one, an FLF6B (Bristol-engined) model with ECW 70-seat bodywork, yet to be repainted red and seen at Scarborough in September 1977, was United's No. **547** (**ANN 566B**), which had come from the East Midland fleet in June 1977 but had started life in 1964 as Mansfield & District No. 646. It was withdrawn and scrapped in October 1979. In the background is a Bristol RE service bus on the sea-front service.

Right: Two years earlier, in September 1975, a Lincolnshire Road Car Company Lodekka is seen in Skegness, demonstrating the NBC's leaf-green and white livery as applied to the former green Tilling fleets. Number **2389** (**OVL 484**), a 1961 FS5G model (and therefore powered by the five-cylinder Gardner engine) with 60-seats and platform doors, was withdrawn and sent for scrap in 1977.

Above: Lincolnshire No. 3019 (**SFU 846**) was one of five vehicles delivered in November 1958 as dual-purpose 41-seaters in cream and green express livery. It was renumbered 2669 in 1962 and in 1970 was converted as a 43-seat service bus and renumbered yet again, as **2069**. In this March 1973 view at Grantham it is still in Tilling green livery although with NBC-style fleetname, evidence of its former express status still visible

in the painted-over beading below the windows. After withdrawal in 1977, this vehicle is believed to have served a farmer as staff transport.

Right: In the early, pre-leaf-green and poppy-red days of the NBC, vehicles were turned out on repaint in the old Tilling shades of green or red. This FS5G Lodekka in the Lincolnshire fleet was photographed in Nottingham in August 1971.

Number **2517** (**VFE 966**) had been beautifully finished: the fleetname transfer positioned below the lower-saloon first window was as carried by both single- and double-deckers in the LRCC fleet at this time. It was withdrawn and scrapped in 1980, as was the Trent vehicle standing next to it. Trent's No. **474** (**ECH 474C**) was an Alexander-bodied 78-seat Daimler CRG6LX Fleetline, one of a batch of ten delivered in 1965.

Above: United Counties No. **207** (**YNV 207J**) was a dual-purpose ECW-bodied 49-seat Bristol RELH6G, one of nine delivered in 1971 and demonstrating how during the first years of the NBC its constituents were still receiving vehicles painted in pre-NBC liveries. The vehicle was brand new in this April 1971 view at Huntingdon Street, Nottingham, with a bright background of Barton vehicles. UCOC No. 207 was transferred to Luton and District Transport Ltd in January 1986 when that company was formed to take over the Luton area of United Counties. The Barton double-decker was No. **736** (**VVO 736**), originally a 1948 Duple-bodied Leyland Tiger PS1/1 39-seat single-decker, rebuilt in 1961 as a Willowbrook-bodied 61-seat double-decker with platform doors.

Right: Two 1974 Bedfords: Barton again shares the limelight with United Counties, this time at Stamford in September 1978. Barton's 1974 Bedford YRT with Duple 53-seat coachwork No. **1316** (**WRR 354M**) was alongside the NBC operator's Bedford YRQ No. **176** (**GNH 530N**), a Willowbrook-bodied 45-seat service bus, one of 27 bought in 1974.

49

Above: Although this West Yorkshire Bristol MW6G is in Tilling red, there are a number of clues that reveal the photograph as being from the NBC-era, most notably the poppy-red Bristol RE alongside. **838 BWY**, with 45-seat ECW service-bus bodywork, was originally numbered SMG30 but was renumbered **1138** in 1971. This photograph was taken at Harrogate in March 1975 and in the following September the bus was sold to the NBC Eastern Region Cannibalisation Centre at Bracebridge Heath, where useful spares were removed before the remains were dismantled for scrap.

Right: This West Yorkshire Bristol FS6B Lodekka, an ECW-bodied 60-seater with platform doors, was one of a batch of 22 delivered in 1961, of which 14 went into the main WY fleet, three were for Keighley-West Yorkshire and five for York-West Yorkshire. Originally DX119, **2015 YG** was renumbered 1719 in 1971 and later **4029** for use as a driver-trainer in 1973, performing those duties for six years until sold for scrap. In this May 1975 photograph, it is seen at Knaresborough.

Above: West Yorkshire's Bristol RELH6G No. **ERG10** (**MWR 962D**) was fitted with Eastern Coach Works 47-seat bodywork and was one of five delivered in 1966. Although fitted with coach seats, it had power-operated folding doors and was regarded as "express" or "dual-purpose" (as suggested by its fleet number), rather than as a coach. In this view taken in August 1970 at Huntingdon Street bus station, Nottingham, it was in use for the Yorkshire Services pool on the London to Leeds service. Before being sold for scrap in 1979, this vehicle was twice renumbered: as 1010 and then 2498.

Right: As part of the celebrations for its 50th anniversary, West Yorkshire repainted a Leyland National in a blue, gold and white livery. Number **1473** (**RYG 765R**), was a 52-seater: one of twelve delivered in 1976/7. In this Harrogate bus station view in September 1978, it is contrasted rather neatly with a National in standard West Yorkshire NBC livery. In August 1989 the vehicle passed to the new West Yorkshire company (owned by Yorkshire Rider), and was then transferred into the Yorkshire Rider fleet in April 1990. It was withdrawn and sold in September 1994.

Above: The East Yorkshire fleet is one of the photographer's great favourites and its vehicles were often recorded on film during summer holidays in Scarborough. Number **739 (3739 KH)** was in the resort's Westwood coach park in June 1971. Named "Bridlington Star", No. 739 was a 1963 Leyland PSU3/3R Leopard with 44-seat coachwork by Thomas Harrington, of Hove. At only 13 years of age the vehicle was dismantled for spares and scrapping at Bracebridge Heath in March 1976.

Right: In the same month and at the same location this picture was taken of East Yorkshire No. **541 (LAT 69)**, a 1950 Leyland PD2/3 Titan with Roe 56-seat body. Since January 1966 it had been in use as a left-luggage office, on which duties it replaced an ex-Everingham Brothers Daimler. Ownership of LAT 69 passed to United Automobile Services in March 1972 and it was withdrawn in January 1975 and sold for preservation, although there have been no reports of it since 1988.

Above: In this June 1974 photograph taken in Leeds, East Yorkshire's No. **858** (**NRH 858F**) is parked between runs on service 44 from Leeds to Bridlington via York, Pocklington and Driffield. It was the first of a batch of eight Marshall-bodied 45-seat Leyland Panther Cubs delivered in 1968. The vehicle lasted a mere ten years and was sold for scrap in October 1978. The livery was a temporary NBC concoction that certainly looked black and white, but was officially stated to be dark blue.

Right: Interim NBC liveries are again evident in this Bridlington photograph taken in September 1973. The single-decker, Leyland PSU3/1R Leopard No. **771** (**9771 RH**) - a Willowbrook-bodied dual-purpose 47-seater - is in the "local coach livery" of blue and white (later to be poppy-red and white). The double-decker, 1963 AEC Bridgemaster No. **748** (**3748 RH**) with Park Royal 72-seat bodywork, was again in the very dark blue and white. On the original of this illustration it is certainly evident that the front mudguards are black and that the body colour is slightly lighter. At the time and on the streets, though, that distinction went unnoticed by many, and this livery was widely referred to as "black and white".

Above: East Yorkshire eventually became a red NBC fleet and the result is epitomised in this study of AEC Renown No. **786** (**CKH 786C**), seen at Scarborough's Valley Bridge bus station in September 1977. The Park Royal-bodied 70-seater was one of a batch of 14 dating from 1965 and was withdrawn and sold for scrap in 1980.

Right: **EHD 966** was an AEC Reliance with Harrington 41-seat coachwork that had entered service with Yorkshire Woollen District as fleet number 852 in 1960. Renumbered 424 in 1967, it was transferred to Hebble Motor Services Ltd on 1st June 1970 along with all of YWD's coach fleet. Renumbered as No. **1** in November 1971, it

was withdrawn in October 1972, two months after this view of it was taken at Chesterfield. The Yorkshire Traction Leyland Leopard alongside is described on page 64.

Above: Unlike East Yorkshire's, many of the red NBC fleets had been red before; thus the new regime involved only a different shade of a familiar colour. One such was the fleet of Yorkshire Traction, whose No. 385 (**FHE 329D**) is seen at Barnsley in June 1975. Originally No. 1329, FHE 329D was a 1966 Leyland Leopard PSU3/3RT, which was when new fitted with a Plaxton 49-seat coach body. After serious accident damage in 1972, it was fitted with this Marshall 53-seat bus body and renumbered 385. Withdrawn in 1981, it passed to the Londonderry & Lough Swilly Railway Company as No. 245. It was reregistered 707 PZO and lasted into the late 1990s.

Right: Taken on the same day in Barnsley, Yorkshire Traction's No. **829** (**HWE 829N**) was a 1975 Bristol VRTSL6G with Eastern Coach Works 77-seat bodywork. In March 1991 it passed to the East Yorkshire group with whom it worked for subsidiary companies until passing into the main EYMS fleet in October 1994, remaining there until sold for scrap in 1996. On this occasion, doubtless, No. 829 returned complete and unscathed from Wombwell, home of several bus scrappers.

Above: In 1969 four Leyland PDR1A/1 Atlanteans were diverted from their originally intended recipient, Devon General, to Yorkshire Traction. Illustrated is the last of the batch, No. **750** (**RHE 450G**). Bodywork was to 75-seat specification by Willowbrook. The photograph was taken at Barnsley in June 1971. The vehicle was withdrawn and sold for scrap in March 1982.

Right: Earlier high-capacity double-deckers in the Yorkshire Traction fleet had been on the traditional Leyland PD3A/1 chassis, of which an example is No. **702** - originally No. 1197 - (**VHE 197**), one of eleven dating from 1961 and seen here still in the operator's pre-NBC livery at Barnsley in May 1970. Behind was No. **712** (**XHE 219**) from the 1962 batch of twelve identical buses and originally No. 1219.

Bodywork, seating 73, was by Northern Counties. These buses were withdrawn in 1973 and 1976 respectively. XHE 219 was scrapped, but VHE 197 went on to have an interesting second career with the China Motor Bus Company, Hong Kong, before being scrapped in 1981. The 8mph speed limit in Barnsley bus station held sway for years but seemed to be "more honour'd in the breach than the observance".

Above: In another view taken in Chesterfield in August 1972 rather more can be seen of Yorkshire Traction's No. **119** (**RHE 119G**) *(see page 59)*. This Plaxton-bodied 41-seat Leyland Leopard PSU4A/4R was one of a pair dating from 1969. Withdrawn in 1980, it was scrapped the following year.

Right: In the previous picture RHE 119G retained Yorkshire Traction's attractive cream and red

coaching livery, in sharp contast with the all-over white seen on another Plaxton-bodied Yorkshire Traction Leopard. Number **874** (**ECK 874E**) had come to the Barnsley operator in June 1978 - one of five transferred from Ribble, with whom they had been part of a batch of 26 bought in 1967 for the Ribble, Scout and Standerwick fleets. Photographed at Barnsley in July 1978, No. 874 was sold for scrap in April 1980. Alongside was

East Midland No. **411** (**411 UNN**), a 1964 Marshall-bodied 53-seat Leyland PSU3/1R Leopard. Recalling the pre-NBC liveries of East Midland and Yorkshire Traction, this picture perhaps more than any other points up the dramatic changes in bus company liveries wrought by the National Bus Company once it got into its "let's repaint everything in different colours" stride.

Above: In 1971 the North Western Road Car Company bought a batch of five Plaxton-bodied Leyland Leopard PSU3A/4R 45-seat coaches. All were altered to 49-seaters soon after delivery; all were transferred to National Travel (North West) Ltd in February 1974 on the break up of North Western and in 1980 to United Counties as Nos 244-8. Number **372** (**SJA 372J**) was at London's Victoria Coach Station in September 1972.

Right: An earlier, 1969, batch of five Leyland Leopard coaches for North Western had been bodied by Alexander as 49-seaters. In this case the batch in its entirety passed to Ribble in October 1973. Number **312** (**NJA 312G**) was at Chesterfield in August 1972, waiting to leave for Manchester on service X67. These coaches were scrapped in 1982 and 1981 respectively.

Above: The PTEs did as much if not more than did the NBC to change the face of British road passenger transport, but there was again an interim period during which familiar liveries continued to appear on new vehicles and later were to be seen side by side with the new PTE colours. The situation in 1971 in Manchester's Piccadilly was typical. Here we see, on the left, a former Manchester Corporation Leyland Titan in the new SELNEC (South East Lancashire North East Cheshire) PTE livery, standing behind a similar vehicle still in Manchester colours. The latter was No. **3466** (**PND 466**), a 1956 Leyland PD2/12 Titan with MCCW 64-seat bodywork. To the right of 3466 was one of the trend-setting "Mancunians", No. **1079** (**LNA 179G**), a Leyland PDR2/1 Atlantean with a Park Royal 76-seat dual-doorway body. In the foreground is a 1965 Manchester Daimler CRG6LX Fleetline with MCCW 75-seat body, No. **4719** (**DNF 719C**).

Right: Former Stockport Corporation No. 51 (**HJA 951E**) is seen as SELNEC No. **5851** at Lower Mosley Street, Manchester, in July 1972. A 1967 Leyland Titan PD2/40, it had bodywork seating 64 by East Lancashire Coachbuilders. It was scrapped in 1980.

Above: In the 1970s foreign buses were far more of a novelty than they have subsequently become. A leader among them was the Scania, which proliferated in both single- and double-deck forms. Leicester City Transport took 98 between 1970 and 1976, of which 35 were single-deck BR111MH models with MCCW 44-seat dual-doorway bodies. Number **138** (**WBC 138J**) was one of the earliest, 1970, deliveries. It was photographed in Leicester in September 1971. The vehicle was withdrawn in 1984 and sold for scrap in 1986.

Right: Neighbouring municipality Derby was a prominent Daimler user from 1936. Roe bodies were specified on CVG6 chassis from 1961 with 52 examples joining the fleet from that year up to 1966. Number **162** (**BCH 162B**) was a 1964 example, with bodywork seating 64, photographed in Derby in April 1972. It was withdrawn in June 1976 and sold to Tiger Coaches, Salsburgh, for scrap. The distinctive Roe patented waistrail can be seen at the point where the cream paint of the upperworks meets the olive green.

Left: West Yorkshire PTE No. **2425** (**PKW 425J**) was a Daimler CRG6LX Fleetline, with Alexander dual-doorway 76-seat bodywork, which had been new to Bradford Corporation as No. 425 in December 1970. It was transferred to the PTE on 1st January 1974. This photograph was taken in Leeds in March 1975. The vehicle was withdrawn by the PTE in 1985.

Right: Nine buses are visible in this August 1971 view of Mount Street bus station, Nottingham. Apart from the Midland General group, Barton and Trent are also represented. In the foreground is Notts & Derby Bristol FLF6G Lodekka No. **573** (**TRB 573F**), an ECW-bodied 70-seater that was new in 1968. In December 1971 it passed to Midland General as No. 306 and then in October 1976 to the Trent Motor Traction Company, with whom it took the fleet number 745. It was sold to an owner in Germany in March 1981. The only other identifiable bus is the single-decker, which was Midland General No. **115** (**BNU 677G**), a 1969 Bristol LH6L with ECW 45-seat bodywork. Renumbered 405 in 1972, it passed to Trent in October 1976 and was sold for scrap in November 1980.

Above: The large companies seldom purchased what were regarded as "lightweight" chassis, and when they did their planned life was often extremely short. Frequently the vehicles went on to serve a subsequent owner for longer than they had their original purchaser. Trent bought a batch of six (Nos 76-81) Bedford VAM5 models, with Duple 41-seat coachwork, in 1967 and all were withdrawn in 1972. This one, No. **78** (**MRC 578E**) went after withdrawal to Lockey, West Auckland, with whom it ran from November 1973 to February 1981. The picture was taken at Huntingdon Street, Nottingham, in June 1971.

Right: Trent No. **169** (**29 DRB**) was a Bristol MW6G with ECW 49-seat dual-purpose coachwork that had been new to Midland General in 1958. Transferred to Trent in 1972, it was withdrawn in 1976 and scrapped the following year. This is a July 1972 picture taken at the bus station in Matlock.

Above: Barton Transport was one of the most photogenic of fleets and was especially attractive when captured on colour film. Number **768** (**URR 868**) was a 1956 Plaxton-bodied 41-seat AEC Reliance. Withdrawn in 1974, it was bought back by Barton for preservation in July 1983. The double-decker behind, No. **795** (**795 BAL**), started life as No. 550 (KAL 147), a Duple-bodied 1948 Leyland Tiger single-decker; it was rebodied as a fully fronted 63-seater by Northern

Counties in 1958 and was withdrawn from service in 1974. A May 1972 picture in Nottingham.

Right: The ultra low-height Dennis Loline that made such a spectacular debut at the 1960 Earls Court Commercial Motor Show was No. **861** (**861 HAL**). Fitted with a Leyland O600 engine and Northern Counties 68-seat body, it was withdrawn in 1973 and remains a member of the "Barton Collection", currently residing at the

Nottingham Heritage Centre, Ruddington. This is a Mount Street bus station, Nottingham, scene taken in June 1975.

Above: Geoffrey Atkins took few rear views; one can be thankful that among them is this fine study of Barton No. **474** (**HVO 135**). A 1947 Leyland PD1 Titan with Duple lowbridge, forward-entrance, 55-seat bodywork, it was withdrawn in August 1971 and sold for scrap. This picture was taken at Broad Marsh bus station, Nottingham, in March 1970. Note the in-house advertising on the side panels and the neat dummy registration-plate

aperture reminding the public that Barton operated a parcels service.

Right: The last double-deckers to enter the Barton fleet came in December 1969 when a pair of ex-City of Oxford Motor Services 1958 Weymann-bodied 65-seat AEC Regent Vs arrived as fleet numbers 1142/3. Number **1142** (**964 CWL**) was photographed at Ilkeston in August 1973 not long before its February 1974 withdrawal, after which it became the company tree-lopper, serving thus until sold for scrap in May 1986.

It seems appropriate to leave this look at the 1970s seen through the photography of Geoffrey Atkins with a colourful view at his favourite bus photography location: Huntingdon Street bus station in his home town of Nottingham. The picture just makes it into our decade, having been taken in June 1970, and everything in it is reassuringly traditional. Every bus has a front engine and a half-cab for the driver, and all are in the liveries that had been associated with their operators for many years. As an image of an era that was about to be succeeded by one bringing radical change, this view could hardly be bettered. On the left is South Notts No. **76** (**76 LNN**), a 1961 Northern Counties-bodied Leyland Titan PD3/6; behind it is another South Notts vehicle and on the far right, next to a just-visible Mansfield District Bristol Lodekka, is Trent No. **417** (**LRC 451**), a PD3/4 Titan with a Willowbrook 73-seat body featuring platform doors. Sandwiched between the South Notts and Trent Titans are two more - a pair from the Barton fleet. **RAL 333** was No. **731**, a 58-seat Leyland-bodied PD2/12 new to Barton in 1954; behind it is No. **942** (**GWW 41**), a PD2/1 with Leyland 53-seat lowbridge bodywork that was acquired from Todmorden Corporation in 1962. This time Barton is using the lower radiator area for its promotional messages.